YOU CAN
IN TELEVISION!

First published in 2002 by Miles Kelly Publishing,
Bardfield Centre, Great Bardfield, Essex CM7 4SL

Printed in Italy

Copyright © Miles Kelly Publishing Ltd 2002

All rights reserved. No part of this publication may be
reproduced, stored in a retrieval system, or transmitted
by any means, electronic, mechanical, photocopying,
recording or otherwise without the prior permission
of the copyright holder.

ISBN 1-84236-096-5

24681097531

Series Editor: Paula Borton
Cover Illustration: The Maltings
Layout Design: Mackerel

YOU CAN MAKE IT... IN TELEVISION!

by Mark Mardell

Illustrations Martin Remphry

Titles in the Series:

You can make it in Television
You can make it in Horse Riding
You can make it in Formula 1
You can make it in Archaeology
You can make it as a DJ
You can make it as a Vet

CONTENTS

YOU'RE ON TV   7

A FOOT IN THE DOOR   20

WALKING AND TALKING   31

THE RIGHT STUFF   45

YOU'RE ON!   82

Mark Mardell is the main political correspondent for the BBC's most watched news programme, *The Six O' Clock News*. Before that he was the Political Editor on BBC 2's *Newsnight* where in his quest to make politics interesting and fun he broadcast from an air balloon, walked amongst computer-generated cartoons and chased a chancellor of the exchequer round a building. He made his TV début standing on the edge of a tall building during Britain's worst gales for a century. He has still not overcome his fear of heights. He began his career at various local radio stations. This is his first book, but he hopes it won't be his last. Mark lives in Surrey with his wife, two children and far too many cats.

YOU'RE ON TV

So what's it really like being on TV then?

There's one thing that never changes.

It's your big moment. You're standing there in front of the camera mumbling to yourself, trying to think of something clever to say. You could be freezing in the Antarctica surrounded by penguins.

You could be sweltering by a camel meat stall in the hustle and bustle of a Middle Eastern market.

You could be talking about the most brilliant scientific discovery.

Or history in the making.

Or how to make a cat basket out of old scarves and empty baked bean cans.

But what happens next is one of the few iron laws of the Universe.

Several small boys on bikes will appear, wheeling around behind you chanting, "Are we going to be on TV, mister?"

It's certain that if you were crouched in your spacesuit ready to broadcast to a waiting Planet Earth – "This is the first time anyone has held the soil of the fabled Red Planet in their hand" – that three bikes would zoom out of the Martian rubble and little green mouths would open to squeak, "Pleazze can we be on television, mister?"

The answer is, "Yeah. It's not easy, but I can tell you how."

It is NOT to turn purple, and run around chasing after the bikes, arms swiping pathetically at the point where small heads were just a moment before, shouting, "Just go on, clear off, I've mucked up that bit fourteen times, my mind's gone blank, we're running out of time and my career is in ruins", before collapsing in a weeping heap. But you can't blame the boys on bikes. Everyone wants to be on TV.

But they didn't really want to be on TV – they were trying to make you cross (and succeeded by the sound of it).

No, they really did. They wanted to point at the TV in the corner of their own living room and say to their mums and dads and friends, "Look that's me on television. It would make them feel real.

Make them feel real? I thought you were going to tell me how to be on TV, not come up with some pretentious garbage about why *I* want to be on the small screen.

No one in the business says "small screen". Look, deep down inside nearly everyone on TV is a little boy or girl jumping up and down, waving, shouting, "Look Mum, look at me, I'm on the telly!"

And it's not very surprising.

That box connects us to the rest of the world.

It might be sad but most people find out more from TV than they ever learn at school or from books.

How do you know what the Spice Girls look like?

How did you find out that Princess Diana had died?

How come you know how to make a cat basket out of old scarves and tin foil?

It could have been a newspaper, or radio, or someone who just told me.

Yes, but I bet you switched on soon afterwards. The wonderful and terrible thing about TV is the way that you can't ignore it.

You know that.

You can be in a room with the most brilliant music playing and the most fascinating conversation going on. But if there's a TV on in the corner, the game's up. That flickering screen draws your eye. Bathed in its light you turn zombie-like and HAVE to watch...

It's not ignorable.

And for a lot of people just being on TV is enough. Not being good, or interesting or funny. Just being on. I've stopped being disappointed when people say to me, "I saw you on the telly, the other day."

You wait for them to say, "and you were making some startlingly intelligent points".

Or, "I disagreed with every word of the incoherent balderdash that you were gabbling".

Or even, "I like the tie with purple flowers on it better than that plain yellow one".

But no. People just say, "I saw you on the telly, the other day". In fact one bloke I often bump into, while wearing my off-duty kit of an old T-shirt and tracksuit bottoms, finally said to me, "You've got a brother who's on the telly, haven't you?" He took some persuading that it was actually me. "Oh," he said sounding a bit disappointed, "you hide it well."

For just to be on the TV means glamour, celebrity, something we can all gossip about at work or school the next day. But they're wrong: it's not just enough to be on the TV. There are some quick ways to get on the TV. They are to be avoided.

DESPERATION CORNER

WAYS TO BE ON TV THAT ARE BEST AVOIDED.

1 Present the Queen or another member of the Royal Family with some flowers. Make sure the event is well covered on local TV. As you rise from your curtsey, your trousers stay behind, exposing a pair of pink frilly knickers. It helps if you are a girl, cute and under eight years old. Although, come to think of it, it would be even more eye-catching if you are male and over fifteen. Bingo! Your humiliation will be replayed on local TV until it is picked up on national TV. Eventually they will stop finding excuses to play the short but excruciating sequence. You will think your agony is over. Just when you are sure nearly everyone has forgotten some bright spark will have an idea for a series called *Ooh What a Cheek!*. People will start giggling at you in the streets again.

2 Have a Terrifying Ordeal. These come in all shapes and sizes. You could be nearly hit by a runaway train. You could be taken hostage in a foreign country for a large part of your life. Those truly fanatical about being on TV could regard the latter option as quite an attractive package. Your friends and family appear quite a lot being tearful before you get released (alongside endless home video footage of you in happier days playing football in the park). On eventual release you will have an emotional news conference at an obscure airport and then an extended interview with someone grave, caring and famous. There is then a good to excellent chance of your own mini series on prisons, religion or friendship with a tie-in book deal. It will also wreck your life and scar you forever.

3 There is one sure-fire way of "being on the telly". Become a small and hideous porcelain ornament of a small girl holding a lamb. Have a dirty lace mat attached to your underside. You will only be removed from the TV for occasional dusting. This is even less attractive than options 1) and 2).

You're just being silly. Aren't you going to tell ME how I should get on the TV?

Sure. Patience is not a virtue in TV.

Here goes then.

Of course, actors are on a lot. But that's cheating. It's not YOU being on the telly, it's just someone you're pretending to be. Which is not to deny that a hefty dollop of natural acting ability comes in very handy...

But let's do a little quiz to see what sort of TV star you might become.

WHO ARE YOU ?

Someone asks you to a party. Do you say:

a) Great, we'll be able to sit in the garden: it's going to be really sunny on Saturday.

b) Great, I'll bring a goat's cheese soufflé with crab sauce.

c) What do you mean, party? Street party? Fancy dress party? "Party" is a pretty imprecise term, isn't it?

d) You smile beautifully and look at the person sitting next to you with great interest.

e) Y'know that reminds me of the story of a boy who'd been away a long time and his dad said let's throw a big party and, like, kill the fatted calf. But his brother was a bit cheesed off. So...

If someone tells you they are going to Florida on holiday, do you:

a) Tell them to watch out for the odd typhoon but say it's mainly very warm, even at night.

b) Recommend they try some 'down home' alligator chilli.

c) Throw yourself back in your chair, look contemptuous and say, "Florida? Everyone goes there. Can't you think of anything more original?"

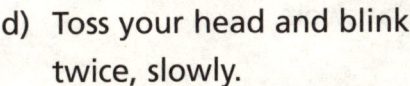

d) Toss your head and blink twice, slowly.

e) Grin and say, "I love holidays but when we think of what it really means, it's not just any old day, it's a special day, it's a HOLY day."

A friend is feeling down after taking a series of gruelling exams. Do you:

a) Tell her that it's usual for lows to follow periods of high pressure.

b) Tell her if she can't stand the heat to get out of the kitchen.

c) Surprise everyone by looking concerned and sympathetic. Then say, "What lessons have you learned from abject failure?"

d) Giggle winningly.

e) Grin and say, "Y'know life often seems like an exam but it's not one where we can blame the teacher: he's already given us all the right answers.

Done?

Mostly As:
Call yourself Bella Brighton-Breasy. You are the sort of person who will easily learn to click on a switch concealed in your left hand while waving wildly with your right hand at a blank green cloth.

Eh? I thought we were talking weather girls?

Or weather boys of course. I'm just making the point that TV isn't always what it seems. Knowing about the weather is just the half of it. The maps you see at home aren't really there in the studio: a computer puts them on. So the real skill is pointing with enough vagueness to the north of England when it isn't there in front of you.

Mostly Bs:
Anyone can chargrill a pepper. But can you do it while talking to a camera and without burning your hand? Better still, can you do it while pretending to burn your hand and yelping theatrically? And then weaving a dire warning about hot grills into a string of amusing chargrilled-

pepper-related anecdotes? If so the tall starched hat of Celebrity Chef Rick Rigatoni is yours.

Mostly Cs:

Prepare to take over from the master inquisitor Simon Sneerman. You are an eagle and politicians are your prey. Read everything, listen to everything and don't believe any of it. You'll have to work on all forty-three facial gestures that say "You're a liar".

Mostly Ds:

Darren Daze and Sara Simper watch out! You could be one of those presenters on Breakfast TV who are there mostly as eye candy. But you can still learn how to ask a clever question. Just repeat what the producer has told you to say through your earphone. The trick is making it sound as though you'd just dreamt it up that second.

Mostly Es:

Be prepared to put on a polo-necked sweater and an informal jacket that's ludicrously out of date. The Sunday late-night religious spot is yours. Percy Priestly can play his TV audience like he plays his battered old acoustic guitar. Which is to say without much subtlety or talent. But he seems happy in his work.

A FOOT IN THE DOOR

So this is the TV studio. It's much bigger than people might think...and much smaller too.

I see what you mean...it's like a big dark cavern littered with cameras and stuff and there's just one little corner with a desk and a couple of pieces of scenery made to look like a bookcase.

And just look up...

Wow!

The ceiling is so high that you can't see it. And those huge big black boxes are very powerful lights. And there's a metal walkway really high up that leads to the gallery, which is where people choose which shots and which cameras to use. Er ...don't mean to be rude, but have you got a name?

I'm Peter Patterson, and I'm mustard keen to appear on your TV screen.

Glad to hear it. Like the name. Although I say so myself, it doesn't hurt to have a snappy name with the initial letters the same.

Alliteration.

Bless you. So you fancy yourself as something of a clever clogs? That's no bad thing.

He's really bright actually. So am I. I think I would be a really good presenter. "This is Daisy Mazey, a little bit crazy ...come on and amaze me."

Argh! You gave me a shock creeping out of the dark like that. Who are you?

I'm just a friend of Peter's. Daisy Mazey. What I think we'll do is if I sit at the desk and Peter sits on that sofa next to it and I start asking questions and then you can tape it or whatever you do and send it off to a few people and then we'll be on TV.

Hang on, Daisy Mazey, you may not be lazy but remember your future's still hazy. Like it? Oh well, the "Daisy Mazey rap" may never make it big-time but if you like I can give you a few tips about TV.

The start is often just getting a job, any job in TV. The lowest rung of the ladder you can find.

OK. Well, I suppose I can't expect to be a big star right away. So I think I'll just be a cameraman. This must be where you stand and I suppose you switch it on with this button ...

Steady on a bit! It takes years of practice and lots of qualifications to operate a camera like that. In fact it needs far more training and qualification than just being on TV. So you can start training on a much simpler piece of equipment. If you peer deep into the darkness of the studio you'll see a sort of carpenter's bench right at the back. See the plastic jug sitting on it? The one with the lead coming out of the back? Well, fill it with water. Stick the lead into the socket in the wall and switch it on. Now in that cupboard you'll find a smallish cardboard box with funny square-shaped bags. Put one in each of the mugs and then pour the boiling water on top of...

Oh I see, you're the man who put the tea into TV. You're being a bit silly, aren't you?

My point is lots and lots of people want to get into TV. Most of them want to start right at the top. And fine if you can do it, that's brilliant. It happens. But most people write loads of letters to everything from that rather old-fashioned regional news programme, *Points West, Looks East*, to the ultra trendy programme makers, *KamraKlub*. Now something slightly eerie is going on. You've got to admit that the programmes they make are pretty different: one specialises in in-depth reports on the Cottsbury by-pass and the other in underwater nude productions of Shakespeare. But the letters they send back are almost identical.

"Sorry, no vacancies" letter

> Dear Mr Patterson,
>
> Thank you for your recent letter seeking employment. Unfortunately there are no vacancies at the moment. However, should a position arise your letter will be kept on file.
>
> Yours sincerely,
>
> The Boss

Well that's good, isn't it? They might write back in a month or two.

I'm sorry. That "file" they're keeping the letter in may be handcrafted leather in one case, and dusty wickerwork in the other, but most of us call it the wastepaper bin.

But if you happen to add that you make a very

decent cuppa, can do it for very little money and have always been the greatest fan of whoever is reading it and that just to hang around in their presence would be an honour... well, then you might have a chance.

The begging letter

Dear Mr Editor,

Ever since I was little I have thought that *Popstars' Pets* was the most brilliant programme on TV. Who'd have thought Westlife would have such a thing about stick insects?

I would love to come and work with you. I've got some free time in the summer holidays and perhaps could watch one of the shows go out and do some odd jobs. My mum says I make the best cup of tea she's ever tasted.

Yours faithfully,
Daisy Mazey

PS I speak five European languages and have a diploma in advanced snake handling which might come in useful if you ever get Emma Bunton to show you her python.

Of course if a TV station will give you a job on your obvious merits that is all to the good, but the most important thing is just being there, getting your foot in the door.

Sorry to bang on about the tea business but there's a pretty well-known TV presenter who was frankly a bit of a nuisance at the radio station where I once worked. He'd come in, hang around the DJs, yes, make them tea, sort their records out (this was in the days when all music came on shiny vinyl) and generally get in the way. He knew a lot about music and all the local clubs so eventually one of the DJs asked him on air to explain who was playing where and whether they were any good.

This grew into a regular Friday evening spot. Then almost to shut him up they gave him what they call the graveyard shift: the show in the middle of the night. The powers that be thought the music he was playing was pretty weird and really they just left him there and forgot about him. That was until someone at the BBC heard him and snapped him up to present a brand new TV music show.

But now you're talking about radio. Isn't it completely different? And can't you get stuck there?

It can be a danger. But not when you are starting out. And Daisy, you have what we call in the business a "radio face". Think about it. No don't think about it... just put the chair down. DOWN. It was only a joke. The skills you need on radio are different from TV, but only a bit and my whole point here is just get your nose into the world of the media. In a radio station you will meet lots of people who do go on TV, whether they are presenters or guests and you can get a good idea what it's like.

And this guy I was talking about? Well, that was nearly twenty years ago. He now gets to go to lots of exotic places to talk about even weirder music in sunny places. He was last seen on Channel Four rabbiting on about how he was voting in the general election. Which proves a point.

It better not be more about tea. While I'm here, though, how do you like it?

Quite strong, no sugar, thanks. The lesson is don't be sniffy about where you start and be prepared to move around a bit. It just so happens that a friend of mine was mentioning that they need a new receptionist at the TV station in Yorkshire where he works.

I'm about to be sniffy.

But the receptionist also doubles as a meeter and greeter. That is one of the two low-level jobs that are worth having. It is exactly what it says, you meet the guests who are coming to be interviewed, make them feel at home and chat to them. You

meet some interesting people if nothing else. In this particular station, like lots of others, people come in to be interviewed by some important national programmes. That happens when there's not enough time to send a camera crew, or they want to do a live interview and the guest can't or won't get to the main studio in time.

Now Peter, race you round the studio.

Why?

To see whether you'd make a good runner.

Well I came second in the 200 metres once but I'm definitely not the next Linford Christie.

Only teasing. Being a runner doesn't have THAT much to do with running. I guess it did in the old days: in the movie business they were the people who ran to get the new cans of film.

Nowadays it really means being an errand boy or girl, taking tapes from one place to another, taking the boss's mobile phone to be mended or getting a vital piece of equipment to the cameraman who unaccountably left it at his last job in a different city (only if you are very, very lucky on a different continent). And almost certainly, I mean I hate to mention this...

A refill? Leave the bag in for a bit longer?

Cheers. The bloke who's the runner at *KamraKlub* is packing it in to go round the world. They've asked him if he knows anybody who'd be good. That's the way it is: you can write all the letters you want but nothing beats knowing someone at the right time. If I put in a good word about your excellent tea-making abilities I'm sure they'd let you have a go.

WALKING AND TALKING

The most amazing thing has happened! You can't beat meeting and greeting! The totally hunky American film star Vincento da Silli was in England for just one night because this friend of his, the lead singer with Ratz, was getting married at his huge mansion. You know, the one in Yorkshire just round the corner from my TV station. That Sunday morning programme, *Sunday's Cool* (try saying it), has been begging him to come on for ages but he just refused to go down to their studio in London. So guess what, as he was so nearby, he agreed to pop in and do what we in the business —

We in the business? Get you.

What we in the business call a "down-the-line interview". That means I had to open up the station, let him in, switch on the big lights, powder him up, sit him down and hit all the right buttons so he could talk to the presenters in London.

How exciting! Hope you were extra careful when you put the earpiece in his right lughole. It's insured for half a million. And I bet he was in a foul mood having to get up so early, and knowing London, they kept him hanging round like a lemon for half an hour.

Bang on! There was this huge mix-up and they wanted him to wait for a whole hour! So I got really cross and shouted down the phone at the director and he sped things up. Vincento was really impressed and grateful. Said I was plucky and determined. And a couple of days later he phoned up and said his friend was the boss of a TV company which was piloting a new pop show and would I come for an interview.

Tomorrow!!!!!!!

Daisy, this is brilliant! You've got a really big chance tomorrow! It would be such a shame if you blew it. I expect they'll get you to do a screen test: see what you look like and how you behave in front of a camera. Mmm. What can I tell you? I'm not sure if you're up to walking.

Funnily enough, I think I can just about manage walking!

Daisy learns to walk.

Well, if you want to start at the deep end, it's up to you. See that camera over there? By the trees? Walk towards it while saying something: I know, just recite the first few lines of "Jack and Jill went up the hill."

" ...and Jill came tumbling after." There, done it!

No, you didn't walk past the camera. You see, next we want to show you by the lake talking about "vinegar and brown paper". We might not film that bit until next Tuesday. Think what it's going to look like. If you walk past the camera we can put both scenes together and it ends up seeming as if you've just strolled from here to the lake.

But if you just stop and then we cut to the shot of you by the lake... well, How did you get there? It'll look as though you've teleported without even the benefit of going all shimmery and hearing Science Fiction music.

It's called a jump cut and it's considered bad news.

You didn't tell me that! OK I'll walk past. "And Jill came tumbling after."

Too quick. When we do this for real we'll be talking about the footballer who lives in the mansion behind you. The cameraman has to have enough time to "pull out" and "reveal" it. In other words make his shot big enough to get the whole building in.

OK. I'll go a bit slower. Jill ...came ...tumbling ...after.

Sorry. Too slow. You were still talking when you'd gone past the camera. That's not a total no-no but there has to be some point to it ...like saying, "I leave you to look at the mansion in all its splendour." I've timed it. You have to do it in twelve seconds. And when you say the words "broke his crown" I want you to gesture back at the building. With your left hand.

"Jill came tumbling around her crown!" Oh no! "Jill came tumbling after." Oh no! I was so busy concentrating on walking I mucked up the words. And it was still too quick. And there's a crowd of stupid people hanging round laughing at me. And it feels funny walking. I'm thinking about where I put my legs. I mean you never ever think about where your legs are when you're walking. Now I can't stop thinking about my legs. I'll never get the hang of this.

Don't worry, you will. You'll even get to ignore the boys on bikes. This is the big problem with TV. You've got to give the impression that you're as cool as a deep-frozen cucumber, that you're almost just larking about while in fact you're doing something very controlled, very precise, and deep down inside you are having half a dozen kittens ...just to keep the butterflies in your stomach company.

You'll do it. But quite a lot of people do get stuck half way.

OK. Maybe we'll leave walking for the time being. How about talking?

Daisy learns to talk.

Talking is a good place to start. As I say, the first time you are likely to be on TV is what we call a "Piece to Camera", or PTC, which the Americans call "a stand-upper", for the obvious reason that you are standing up and talking to the camera when you do it. Americans know a lot about sounding chatty and matey. And that's what you're after. They also get bonus points, from our point of view (that's POV in TV terms) for being much nicer towards people on telly. Camera crews in the States will call you "The Talent". Here in Britain you get called "The Lips" if you're lucky or "The Gob on a Stick" if you're not.

Talking, like walking, on TV can feel like an unnatural act. This is because it is unnatural. After all you are trying to display your enthusiasm and knowledge to a round black lens that stares back at you unblinking and unforgiving.

Sounds like you're trying to put the wind up me. What do I do ...give it a long hard — what was it — unblinking stare back?

No, talk to someone else. A cameraman I know has a small but very attractive teddy bear taped to the top of his camera. He tells people we're interviewing to talk to that. He gets some odd looks, but he gets some results as well.

I'm not convinced talking to teddy bears is the answer, but imagine you're chatting to one person, and have them in the back of your mind. A friend, your brother. I think of my mum. But I wouldn't want to overdo it. Leave waving and saying "Hello Mum!" to the boys on the bike.

Why do you have to do this? It all sounds a bit babyish, pretending you're talking to a toy or your mother.

Partly so you sound like you're having a chat with someone you know. Otherwise a lot of people either sound like they're addressing a school assembly or lecturing a very stupid two year-old.

But the main reason is to make you feel more comfortable. How did it feel at the end of your walking lesson?

Really terrible. I mean, I didn't think I would be nervous, but then my mouth was all dry, and I felt like everyone in the world was looking at me and ready to criticise if I got the slightest thing wrong and then I had to do it over and over again. And I started to forget the words even though it was only a stupid nursery rhyme.

Exactly. What you don't want to think about is the millions of people on the other side of that cold lens.

I'm going to tell you something that you should never EVER think about again.

There are programmes, mostly on in the middle of the night or on rather worthy subjects, of which people in the business will say lightly, "Oh, no one ever watches that!"

In fact if the audience is below a certain number of people they don't bother to write down the exact figure.

That figure is half a million people.

So if you end up working for a show "No one ever watches" it's the same as if you are standing at the centre of a football stadium and every man, woman and child who lives in the city of Bristol is waiting for you to speak.

Now forget that...

I'll give you a little tip I've never passed on to anyone else because it's a bit embarrassing. Look at the camera and think, "This camera really loves me more than anyone else in the world, in fact it fancies me so much... it's just hanging on my every word, really wanting me to do well."

And that will get rid of the nerves?

No, I'm afraid only time and practice will do that. The first time you are waiting to go live your heart will feel like it's going to burst out of your chest, as if it couldn't go any faster. That's until you actually do start speaking and it'll move to the middle of your throat and you'll feel so dizzy you'll have to stop yourself swaying from side to side. The next time it's better. And better. Until it feels like something you do every day. By that time it probably will because it IS something you do every day.

It all sounds a bit like hard work.

Just trying to scare you. But there is one last thing you could try.

Now what?!

No, this will be fun. Or rather, if you don't find it fun at all you really wouldn't like working in TV. A lot of the things said on TV are written beforehand. The skill is, again, trying to make it appear as if they're not. As if they are normal speech. You're lucky: you haven't been spoilt by too much education.

Are you taking the... ?

In a word, yes. But you must have heard some people on TV who are really trying hard to use clever words and in the end they just sound stuck-up and out of touch. I don't think they've got to you yet. You're unspoilt.

So I just say what comes naturally?

Well, you want to watch that. There's a dreadful

disease that some reporters catch which is officialitis. Its symptoms are swallowing the words of some star's publicist or the police or whoever, and regurgitating them a short time later.

The other day I heard a normally very good reporter say some people had "access to an array of armaments". He wouldn't go home and tell a friend that. He'd say, "They could get their hands on loads of guns." But he'd been given the information by an American policeman so ended up sounding like an American policeman.

So here's the homework. And, as they say, you can do this at home. Think of a subject. It doesn't really matter what. The view out of your bedroom window. Your journey to school. Your best friend's face. What you thought of the last book you read. Now write something down. Not much, half a page, a page of an exercise book.

Then put it to one side and get an old tape recorder. Or a brand new one, for that matter. Or better still, a video recorder. Thinking of the same subject, just talk about it for a couple of minutes. It doesn't matter at all if you um and er and hesitate and stumble and stop. Just do it.

Then write it out (without the ums and the ers). Then read both of them out loud. Bet you which one sounds more natural. The written one might be better English but it won't sound as good. (The computer I'm writing this on keeps bossily underlining my sentences in green and telling me they are "ungrammatical fragments". Computers may not like it but most people speak in "ungrammatical fragments".)

There's another problem about writing for TV, which you can test out for yourself using the video recorder. One of the stories people who work in radio love to tell is of the little girl who was asked whether she liked radio or TV best. She is meant to have replied, "Radio. The pictures are better." Radio people love the story because it means their writing fired up her imagination, painted a picture in her mind. In TV you can't do that: the pictures are painted by, well, pictures.

So a radio script would be....

There's a boy in a black baseball cap skateboarding down the road. Oh NO! He's wobbling all over from left to right. To make it worse he's got a big ice-cream cone in each hand. There's a terrified old lady and her poodle running in the opposite direction. Too late! They've crashed. She's got one cone in the eye and he's got the other one stuck on top of his head. And the poodle's trying to lick it off both of them."

OK, eh? You get the picture, don't you? Well that's the problem. On TV you've already got the pictures. So you have to add to what the pictures are telling you but not ignore them.

So a TV script is...

Shot of Billy with two ice-creams: *Cool. Billy's found a way of chilling out and keeping the temperature down.*

Shot of Billy wobbling: *But it doesn't look as if a cornetto in each hand is the ideal way to keep his equilibrium.*

Shot of lady and dog running away: *Now Mrs Smith knows what running scared really means: look at her face.*

Cut to dog about to trip up
Billy: *Lead on, Rover. But that's the trouble: his lead's still on and it's tight as a trip wire.*

The crash: *We now do what is known as "Let the pictures breath". It means don't talk when something really interesting is happening.*

Shot of dog licking ice-creams: *And on a hot day what could be nicer for Rover than a spot of raspberry ice-cream? But I wonder where the flake ended up?*

A bit cheesy. So half the time you're just telling people where to look. But you're always banging on about keeping it simple: do you really think everyone knows what "equilibrium" means?

No. But it's the only word that means both "keeping his cool" and "keeping his balance" and when the pictures are that good you can sneak one in.

THE RIGHT STUFF

So Daisy got the job. It's all right for some, isn't it? This running is all very well but I've been doing it for a year now and I didn't go to college and everything to be a glorified errand boy.

No, don't be like that, Peter. The whole business is full of ups and downs, unexpected breaks, less thrilling but equally unexpected reversals. That's what makes it so great: more like a game than a job.

In the business I believe we call that a cue...

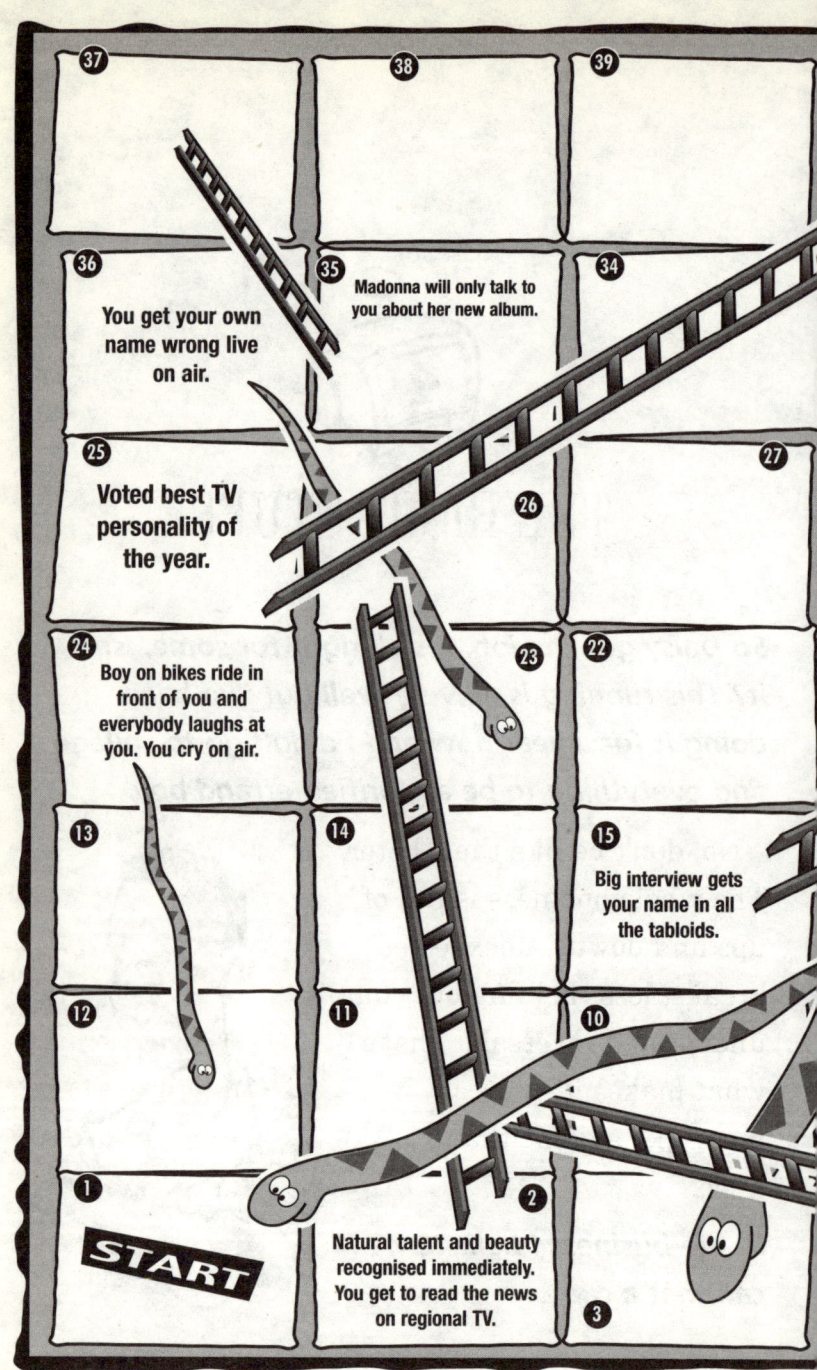

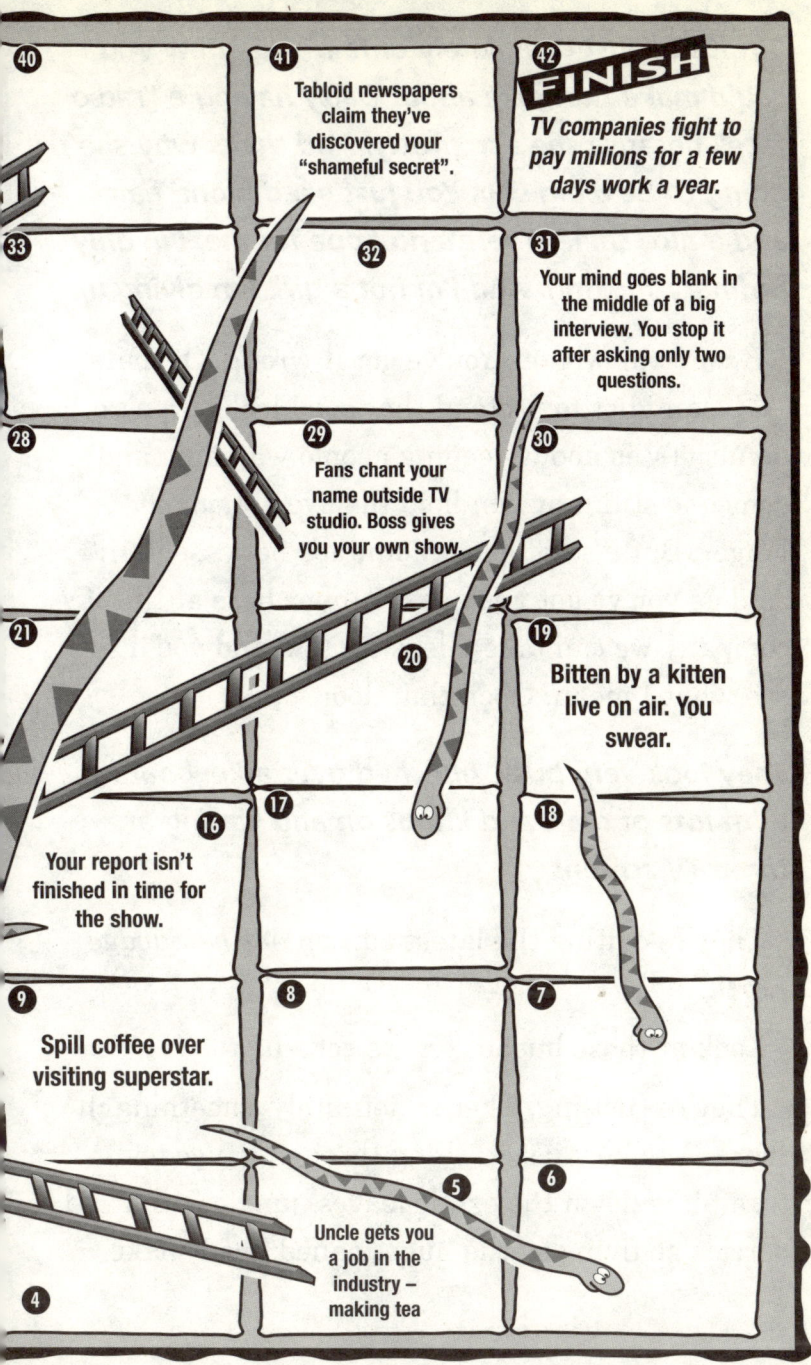

But it's all just completely unfair. You knew you could make that joke about Daisy having a "radio face" because she's so pretty. And that's why she's going to be a big star. You just need blond hair and a nice smile. There's no hope for me, I'm only ordinary-looking. And I'm not a girl. I'm giving up.

Keep your wig on. You've got it wrong. Of course I'd be an idiot to pretend that good looks aren't a bonus. TV is about keeping people watching and someone stunning can hold the eye a moment longer. But it's not enough and it's not essential. And as you've got a job as a runner here at this TV company we can take a look around and you'll soon see what I mean. Open that door.

They look very busy, hunched over a keyboard with lots of dials and knobs on and staring at three TV screens.

They're editing the latest edition of *The Savage Earth*.

Look at those bushes on the screen.

They're rustling. There's definitely something in there. And now it's crashing through. Huge feet trampling down the exotic leaves, jungle fruits and berries go flying as the huge-maned head shakes and as the mouth opens spittle flies from its twisted sharp teeth.

Then Jack Savage speaks his by now famous opening lines:

"This is *The Savage Earth*. With me, Jack Savage ...and from here it only gets wilder. Now let's have a look at this fantastic fabuloso little creature I've got here."

He opens a large, red and none-too-clean hand to reveal a wriggling scorpion. Now, Jack stands six-foot-four from the tip of his yellowing toenails to the top of his knotted hair, from where a stick insect from the last series is struggling to escape.

His tummy is having an equally ferocious but slightly more successful battle with his over-tight khaki shirt. The bits of belly that have made it through the buttons to the outside world are as uninviting and as translucently pale as the Mahargretti grubs he ate in the previous programme.

In other words Jack isn't exactly prime material for lead singer in a boy band. His poster is not on many bedroom walls. But he knows everything there is to know about anything nasty and slimy that stings and by the end of the programme you know a fair amount about them too.

Where next? That red light means they're on live, should we go in there?

It's OK. Now underneath that rather absurd three-foot-high starched white chef's hat is Dilly Doughnut. Look at the speed of her knife as she carves into that mango.

But she's perfectly normal-looking. She hasn't got vast hairy knees like Jack Savage. At least I don't think so... I can't see underneath the blue and white apron.

No, and they don't have to disinfect the whole studio with a cloud of insecticide when she leaves, either. But you said it... she's perfectly normal-looking. Nothing special, you wouldn't look twice at her in the street. Bit like a female version of you, really. Just ordinary. But listen, and look.

Dilly's knife flashes as she talks, turning the innocent fruit on her chopping board into a series of perfect little circles about the size of a pound coin. She is saying, "What I just *ADORE* about this **GORGEOUS** fruit is the smell and the juice. I wish you could smell the aroma that is WAFTING as I slice... Heady! It just says 'India'. Now we're going to put those lovely little mounds into a dish to join the rest of our fruit salad in a moment. But here's a little secret. Just get the mango stone, hold it over a bowl, and **SQUEEZE!** Squish, squish squish!!"

"Just imagine you are squeezing out a damp swimming costume! Or I always think of my producer's neck!" Dilly grins a wide and frightening grin.

Wow. She's seriously weird. I never thought you could make the word "neck" last for fifteen seconds.

She is weird. But she's a star. You have absolutely no interest in making a fruit salad, have you? But you were gripped; if you were watching at home you wouldn't have turned over. And I bet you'll never wring out your swimming trunks again without thinking of mangoes.

That's an achievement?

That's the power of TV. Let's just go outside into the street for a moment. I need some fresh air after all that mango.

Look, look. That's Davey Hart!

What, that fat kid with the bucked teeth in an outsized chequed suit? And a big afro wig? The one prancing around in front of the camera clutching a pile of letters?

I can't believe you don't know who he is! He does Hart to Heart *every morning of the school holidays. It's sort of like a problem page, only it's not really serious stuff and he phones people up and makes them talk to each other if they've split up. And he puts on this silly deep voice for this catch-phrase he's got – "Are you in a deeeeep, lurve grooooove?" He's so funny and sometimes he turns up on people's doorsteps when they aren't expecting him. And the other morning he made this couple KISS on air for the first time!*

Not what you'd call a looker? Not a blond hair in sight? It's certainly a smile, but it's not a pretty one.

No, but he just cracks me up. "Are you in a deeep lurve grooooove?" It's mad, its great.

We've got that straight then. None of these three people are on TV BECAUSE of their looks. And two of them are downright repulsive. But Davey and Jack have been clever enough to make the most of the way they look, and not by going to beauty parlours and style consultants. But what do they all have in common?

Loud voices?

Now you mention it, yes. But they all really know what they're talking about and have a passion for it. Maybe Davey doesn't have a lurrvve degree but Dilly was a top chef before she was ever on TV and Jack has his own zoo.

But that's not enough, either. Look at Derek the diver. He regularly plummets to near the bottom of the Pacific Ocean. He's seen tropical fish so weird that science refuses to describe them. He's swum in and out of sunken galleons a-glitter with pirate gold in a dozen different seas.

And he's most certainly not on TV. He drives people away at parties with his talk of the competing demands of water-resistance drag

versus insulation density in rubber diving suits and the necessary coefficient in pressure-to-light ratios in an on-going diving situation. He's a bore.

Davey and Jack and Dilly want you to understand their passion. If they didn't tell the world about it, they'd burst. They have character. They might even have a little poetry in their soul.

But I still haven't got a decent job, have I?

Maybe patience is a virtue, even in TV.

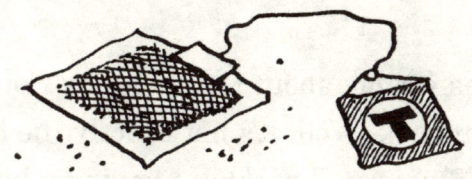

IN THE FAST LANE

Peter, I was wrong, about those letters! Someone has written back. Well, it's not exactly the big break but *Stardust Tonight* are having a bit of a crisis. Their main reporter can't get a flight back from America, two have gone off sick and their researcher has simply disappeared. They're offering you a couple of days as a stand-in reporter. Not that you'll probably end up doing much.

I think what you said to Daisy has put me off. Heart about to burst, end up so you don't even know how to walk, the terrifying lens staring at you? You make it sound like the scariest job in the world.

"It's only television" some people say. It can be an

excuse but it does make the point that when a brain surgeon or a coach driver makes a big mistake the result is more serious than someone looking silly.

But as for lonely? No. Crowding behind that camera is a whole team. It's your face on the screen. It's your name people might recognise. If the team make a mistake people watching think it's your fault. Equally you'll get the credit if they do something brilliant.

The team can be the best thing about work in TV. So let's meet some of them.

Here's the cameraman. (There are lots of camerawomen now but no one's thought of a good word to cover both sexes). If he sometimes looks a bit grumpy that's because in the last few years he's been turned into what we call "a one-man band".

I can't see a drum on the back or an accordion strapped to his front but he looks pretty weighed down!

Yes, not long ago he'd have had three or four people to help. There could be a sound recordist, a lighting man, sometimes a film assistant. A film assistant in the days of using real film instead of videotape, used to carry around a big black bag made of thick cloth. His job was to cover the camera with the bag and fiddle around to change the film so the light didn't get in and ruin it.

Now this chap coming towards us with the pained expression is carrying not only his camera, but the "legs" or "sticks" (camera tripod), a couple of lights on long poles, a big zeppelin-shaped microphone also on a pole, and batteries the size of dictionaries that weigh half a tonne.

QUICK CAMERA QUIZ

It's vital to get on with the cameraman. So how would you do?

When you see him stagger over the horizon, what do you say?

a) That looks really heavy. I'm glad I'm a reporter and don't have to lug gear around like some technician.

b) Oh, you shouldn't have to carry all that. Can I take some of it?

c) Hello, mate. Shall I take the legs?

You are waiting to do a piece to camera and the cameraman is messing around with the equipment. Do you:

a) Keep looking at your watch and sighing. Eventually say, "What's the delay, has something broken?"

b) Say, "Shouldn't we do a 'White balance'?" Unless you show the camera something white and adjust for the light we are in, all the other colours will look most strange.

c) Hold up your open notebook and say, "Do you need to do a 'white'?"

The cameraman is taking a long time to perfect a really fiddly shot which involves zooming out of close-up shots of a skyscraper to reveal the whole city skyline.

Do you say:

a) Come on. Surely we've got enough pictures. Anyway it's what I say over them that's important.

b) Why don't you pan from left to right before picking up the sign on the top of the skyscraper and THEN zoom out? You could try to get that seagull in the shot as well.

c) That's great. I bet it'll look really good. Did you get a shot of the skyscraper on its own?

Mostly As:

As far as cameramen are concerned you are a typical reporter. Someone who ponces around in front of a camera they haven't got enough intelligence to operate but who think they're the best thing since sliced bread, just because they don't have to twiddle any knobs. Someone who doesn't realise TV is all about pictures. There are many

"mostly As" around and cameramen go out of their way to humiliate them.

Mostly Bs:
There is such a thing as too keen. Cameramen are deeply suspicious of young pups who think they know the job better than them. But they'll be happy to let you carry the two bags of batteries that weigh as much as a small car, as well as a couple of tripods.

Mostly Cs:
You realise that it's the cameraman who makes the difference between something shoddy and almost unbroadcastable and something that some people will call art.

Now, the most annoying bit about being on TV is when someone says, "But you were only on for a couple of minutes. What do you do all day?" This is what you do all day:

PETER PATTERSON'S DAY IN THE LIFE OF A CUB REPORTER.

PART ONE

You've gone to bed early the previous night to be ready to go into the office bright and early at nine o' clock. That's what you think.

2.00 a.m.: Your phone rings. Your bleep goes off. Your mobile phone starts trilling.

Your editor tells you that the film star Vincento da Silli is in London for the premier of his new film, *The Mask of Destiny* but he's gone into hiding after all the critics said it's completely pretentious rubbish and he's lost his edge. He hit a very distinguished film critic in a restaurant last night. The police might want to speak to him. The editor says,

"I want my best reporter outside the hotel where we think he's staying."

Your heart swells with pride.

"So I've sent him there. I want you to stake out another place down the road where's he been in the past. I'm pretty sure he's not there and it's a waste of time but I can't take the risk.

3.30 a.m.: Vaguely washed and dressed you stumble into a taxi.

4.00 a.m.: Arrive at the hotel. You meet your cameraman, Ian. He's lean and spry and tanned, enveloped in a big khaki waistcoat that seems to be made up entirely of little pockets. Screwdrivers, pliers and less identifiable tools poke out of the top of them. Round his middle is a big blue webbing belt holding spare batteries. He's wearing baggy shorts, hiking boots and knee-length white socks. But you can't have everything.

4.30 a.m.: A flurry of excitement as there's movement inside the hotel. Ian shoulders his camera. You rush forward with a microphone. You shout, "What do you think of the critics?" A middle-aged Japanese businessman looks startled as he hails a taxi for his early morning flight back to Tokyo.

5.00 a.m.: Some early staff start arriving at the hotel. They've heard a rumour that Da Silli is staying there.

5.20 a.m.: You are begining to have a good feeling about Ian. He's just back from covering a small war in the Middle East, and immediately before that shot several episodes of *The Savage Earth* in Borneo. But he doesn't seem disgruntled to be working with you, outside a hotel and this unearthly hour. He's a pro.

5.45 a.m.: A reporter from the Press Association arrives.

6.10 a.m.: Your rival from another TV station arrives. He is immaculately turned out. His tie cost more than his suit and that cost more than you'll be paid in a month. He has "Mostly As" written all over him. Trailing behind in the wake of this star's floral aftershave is the cameraman. He's called Sid but most people who work with him call him something with a few more letters. Overburdened with gear he looks as though he got dressed in the dark. He probably did. His tatty and necessarily very large pair of jeans don't really go with the pale green nylon shirt. Neither match the cheap kagoul. He grumbles constantly about being up this early, his back and the state of the world today.

7.00 a.m.: More people are coming and going from the hotel but no one has heard anything about Da Silli.

7.20 a.m.: Your cameraman, Ian, has just shot a piece to camera with the building looming over your left shoulder. The light is right, catching your good side, and the building looks even posher than it really is. In short he's made you look fabulous.

7.30 a.m.: Ian persuades the reporter from the press association to go and get some coffee and a bacon sandwich with a promise we'll cover for him if anything happens.

8.00 a.m.: Eat bacon sandwich.

8.30 a.m.: Sid shoots piece to camera with his "talent". (He definitely calls him the "Gob on a Stick".) When they come to look back at it for all his expensive suit your rival looks as though he's been dipped in blue ink. Sid forgot the white balance. And because he didn't offer to carry any equipment Sid didn't tell him that he had bacon grease dripping down his posh tie. Just out of spite he's shot him at a weird low angle that makes him look like he's got three chins and a tree growing out of his head.

But Sid can muck things up even when he likes you. He really isn't much cop.

9.00 a.m.: Wonder how cold your feet can get. Try some walking up and down.

9.30 a.m.: Ring the office to ask if they want you to stay here. They do.

10.10 a.m.: Listen to Sid's views on "the Government" to see if it relieves the boredom. It doesn't.

10.30 a.m.: Wonder if you've made a career mistake. Surely even all-night security guards get somewhere warm to sit down?

11.17 a.m.: You spot something happening by the rubbish bins. So has Ian. He's been looking around him all this time and has noticed something weird going on.

Sid is moaning to the man from the Press Association about working on a Saturday and is staring mournfully at the grouts of coffee at the bottom of his Styrofoam cup.

11.18 a.m.: Ian races down there, you follow him closely, camera bobbing on his shoulder. He stops and holds really still, gets a nice shot of Vincento being pushed out in a wheelie bin surrounded by heaps of discarded cauliflower and covering his face with a carrot-adorned beanie hat.

Your rival realises something is going on and starts shouting at Sid.

11.21 a.m.: Ian then drops to his knees to get superbly silly shot of the vegetable-crowned star being poured into the back of his stretch limo. Then he pulls out, widens the shot... so he gets you in the picture as well.

Sid tries to turn his camera round to point in the right direction but it's firmly attached to the tripod so he can only see the back of you, the PA reporter and Ian.

11.21 a.m.: and thirty-two seconds: Ian has switched on the microphone so the world hears you shouting, "Vincento, is your latest film as bad as all the critics say?"

Sid has wrestled his camera from its tripod and has it on his shoulder. He lumbers in the right direction. But he's got the wrong microphone switched on so you can only faintly hear Vincento say, "It's my greatest masterpiece. The critics can go stuff themselves. And I'll belt anyone else who disagrees!!"

11.22 a.m.: Ian turns back towards Sid and gets a shot of him. Why? It's called a cut-away and all the other pictures are useless without them. Why? When we meet the editor he'll bore you stupid about it. Sid gets a shot of the departing limo. It's the only useable shot that he's got. But no, it's not useable because he's forgotten to get any cutaways.

11.25 a.m.: It's all over. A doorstep of more than seven hours for five minutes of intense action. That's TV. Sid and his reporter are hunched over their camera pushing and shoving to get a look through the eyepiece. They're looking back at what few pictures they have. You leave before the harsh words turn to blows. That's TV. About all Sid will get on TV tonight is his own bewildered face in Ian's cut-away.

Time for a lunch break. Over lunch you can meet some more of the team.

All this time someone else has been your discreet shadow, staying slightly back from all the action but no more than a glance away.

Yes. She's now the next most important person in your life. The producer. If they're just starting out and only do the more menial bits of the job they could be called fixers or researchers.

It doesn't matter what they're called. They're your best friend, your nursemaid, your dogsbody and your better half. You know that game where you fall straight backwards and have to hope the person behind will catch you? That's what it's like with a good producer: they've earned your trust enough to do the riskiest things. Actually that's what it's like with a bad one as well. You think, "Oh no! Where on earth have they got to!" moments before your head hits the floor with a sickening thud. Only you make sure you don't play that game with that friend again. But with a bad producer you don't always have the choice and just have to get used to constant headaches.

It's difficult to describe what they do because

they should be able to do the lot, from booking taxis to sweet talking presidents. A good producer will work out what bits you're good at and let you get on with it, and then they'll fill in the gaps. With some "talent" that means they end up doing everything from writing the script to tying shoelaces.

This on top of ordering taxis, paying bills, and their real job of talking over what we're going to do, how we're going to do it and when. Their job at its most basic is telling you when you are wrong, so this can lead to a lot of deep sighs and raised eyebrows on both sides leading sometimes to stomping off and the slamming of doors. Someone I know calls all his producers of either sex "The girlfriend" on the grounds he spends more time with them than his actual partner. You end up talking about them admiringly when they're not around and missing them like crazy, but when you are actually together you spend all the time arguing and patching up rows.

Here's someone else. You won't be working with him today but it's worth saying hello.

Strangely this is some one who hardly exists anymore. Terry the Sparks was almost made extinct when cameramen became "one-man bands".

His job went. But he didn't. Terry has a gold bracelet, a gold watch, a gold medallion and a heart of ...well, he picked it up in Hong Kong on the cheap and you'd never tell it from the real thing. "Look at that, Guv ...you could never tell, could ya? If you fancy one I've got this mate..." In the old days the sparks was the person who did the lighting (in normal speech it's the electrician).

He'd joke that he never travels without two blondes and a redhead. They are nicknames for

kinds of lights but seeing it was probably a sparks who first gave them the nickname you can see how his mind works.

Up until the mid-1980s even a simple interview inside needed two or three big, heavy, hot lights and it was the sparks' job to set them up before the cameraman fiddled with them in a fussy sort of way.

They don't do that now but you need to know about them because, although the job has gone, people like Terry found themselves new roles as cameramen, producers or tape editors. But inside he's still a sparks.

When a senior female politician is being very difficult and frosty about giving an interview because someone forgot to call her "Lady Muck" rather than Mrs Muck, Terry will turn up, fling his arms around her, say "Gawd you haven't changed, luv". It'll turn out that 12 years ago they spent a night drinking sherry and stout cocktails in a Brighton hotel during a political conference. The ice is broken and you get the interview.

When you can't get into that nightclub to film the dance floor, where a pop star known for her dancing twisted her ankle, it will turn out that the bouncer owes Terry's bruvver-in-law a favour.

When you've worked a 28 hour day and the producer hasn't booked a hotel and they're all full up, Terry will charm the receptionist and slip her free tickets to *Popstars' Pets* to get you all in. And when you've all been celebrating your triumphs too long and too hard Terry will guide you to the van and drive you all home. *And* find a parking space.

The last member of the team is the tape editor.

Like many of the breed Dave is pale and a bit gloomy. He's rarely allowed out of his darkened and windowless basement room. When he does escape it's not much better. On exciting foreign trips to exotic locations, while everyone else charges around admiring the view, he stays in his hotel room with the curtains drawn only seeing palm trees and sand on the tiny TV sets that are the tools of his trade. The only alternative to this is to become a "shoot-edit" which means being both editor and cameraman. This is great if you have an insatiable desire to combine two stressful jobs and start doing the second one just when you're really, really tired from doing the first.

The ways of doing it have changed. With film you physically cut one piece of tape and stick it on to the next bit. The hunt for the bit you thought was hanging round your neck but turns out to be somewhere among all the other lengths of film on the floor can be a challenging moment to those likely to throw temper tantrums. For most of us these days it's a question of copying one videotape on to another one although increasingly it's done on a computer.

And cut-aways? You might think it odd that news programmes will often show a shot of cameramen or photographers. Or for that matter during an interview you suddenly see the shot of a reporter listening intently (these are called "noddies" because most people try to nod encouragingly but end up looking like one of those toy dogs on the back window of cars). This is taken after the real event and the idea is to move smoothly between one bit of the action and the next. If we hadn't got that shot of Sid the cameraman looking perplexed we'd have had to cut from Vincento in the bin, to Vincento shouting from the car, and that would look silly, like a jump in time. The only alternative would be to use all the pictures in between but that went on for four minutes and you've only been given three for your whole report.

PETER PATTERSON'S DAY IN THE LIFE OF A CUB REPORTER.

PART TWO

1.00 p.m.: You return to the office. No ticker tape, no champagne but they seem relieved you've got the shots of Vincento and no one else has.

2.00 p.m.: Programme meeting to decide what goes in tonight's show. Huge row about whether they should interview the critic Vincento hit. They decide against it.

They've given you three minutes to do the report. That's quite long. Most news pieces are 75 seconds.

2.20 p.m.: Big row with the producer about how to start the piece.

2.40 p.m.: You say, "But it's my piece." It is. But she wins.

3.00 p.m.: You write a rough structure for the piece. It goes like this:

> Slo mo ...Vincento in rubbish bin. Track says something like, "Is this the moment the pressure got too much for Vincento da Silli?" Joke about load of rubbish.
>
> Clip from Mask of Destiny: Da Silli saying, "This

> is the mask of destiny ... Over picture of him holding up mask,
> Script about what the critics said.
> (Note to producer: should we use graphic of quotes from critics here??)
> Shot of restaurant where he hit the critic.
> Interview with critic (producer did this: V. keen we use). "He has every right to be annoyed ...annoyed with himself for appearing in such garbage."
> Patterson piece to camera ... it's here at this hotel etc.
> Link into shots of Vincento emerging from hotel.
> My shouted question and his answer.
> Shot of limo driving off ...thought about "Is this the last we'll see of the temperamental star?"

3.10 p.m.: Go into the edit suite. First thing Dave says is: "Got any cut-aways?"

You have. He looks through the pictures.

3.15 p.m.: You write the script and go to record it back in the edit suite.

4.00 p.m: Start the edit. The show goes out at seven and cutting three minutes in three hours is giving you a bit of spare time.

Dave puts your voice down on tape and then

he puts the pictures over to match. Big row about what shots to use where.

5.00 p.m.: You've cut the first thirty seconds but are still waiting for a clip from *Mask of Destiny* (the film that caused all the trouble) to arrive from the film company.

5.20 p.m: Still waiting. You have to start editing the rest of the piece on a different tape!

5.55 p.m.: Dave is in a controlled panic. He looks like a virtuoso pianist hammering his keys and buttons.

6.15 p.m.: Disaster! The film company won't let you use any of the film because you won't promise to be nice about Vincento. The producer has to find an old report she shot about the making of the film and use that instead.

6.30 p.m.: You've done it! With time to spare!

6.34 p.m.: Oh no you haven't! The boss of the programme rings up. He's decided to interview the critic live after all. So you can't have him in your piece. You have to find something else.

6.36 p.m.: Luckily the producer also did an interview with a waiter who saw the fight. And he's quite funny. "If he threw punches like that in his film the bad guys would think a girl was stroking their cheek." Yet again you have to re-write and re-edit the whole section.

6.47 p.m. A man appears at the door and asks if you've finished. NO!!

6.52 p.m: The editor rings and asks if you're going to make it. Yes. Don't know. Maybe.

6.56 p.m.: You're finished. The man at the door takes the tape and runs. You turn to the producer and Dave and say, "Please tell me it's not always like this." They look at each other and say together: "It's ALWAYS like this!"

6.59 p.m.: But it's been a good day. Treat yourself. Switch on the TV. It's a moment you'll remember. The opening music of *Stardust Tonight* comes on and a grinning Tracy Toppit announces, over Ian's brilliant pictures.

"It's where the critics put him ...in the bin. But Vincento tells our own Peter Patterson why his latest film isn't a load of old rubbish!"

Now quickly hit the remote. On the rival channel, they're playing Sid's dreadful shot of the limo disappearing. You can faintly hear the voice of your rival shouting to his cameraman, "You klutz! How the hell did you miss Vincento speaking!" Then four earnest men try to discuss the star's strange behaviour, but they're struggling without pictures of the vegetable-covered star. Sweet, eh? Go on, give in, and gloat. But remember while you get the fame and glory, it's only because Ian has done the real work today. Without his pictures you wouldn't even have had a story.

You're only as good as your team. So buy him a big bottle of something and give the rest of them your heart-felt thanks.

YOUR'E ON!

Remember that big studio at the beginning? Daisy is in it. Live on air.

In a moment we'll be meeting the boys who put the lawnmower back in Garage...Yes, after the break I'll be talking to The Bad Blades... the two razor-sharp DJs who are supporting Ratz on their latest tour.

Doesn't she look cool, doesn't she look fabulous? But she didn't just swan in before the big red light went on. This is what it takes:

Daisy's Morning

4.45 a.m.: Get Up. Late already.

5.00 a.m.: No time to change properly. Put some of my new outfits in a bag and sling on an old pair of jeans and a T-shirt.

5.05 a.m.: Taxi driver picking me up says," Hello gorgeous". Don't feel gorgeous. Yet.

5.30 a.m.: Programme meeting. Run through what we're doing on the show.

6.00 a.m.: Change in to a really smart but simple blue mohair dress. A little bit on the expensive side but what the heck!

6.10 a.m.: Programme Editor says my lovely new dress "is not the image the show is trying to project". Will have to change.

6.30 a.m.: Script conference. Look at scripts written for me. Change them a bit.

7.00 a.m.: Try on my "summer special", a rather daring low-cut designer top in aquamarine with mini skirt made from

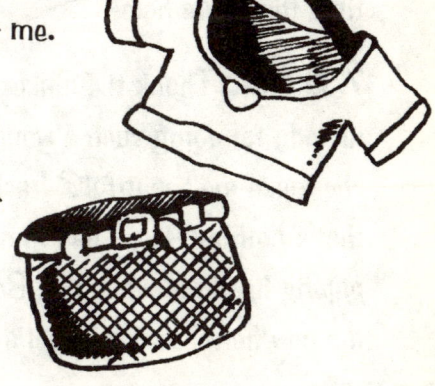

seagrass. Ironically tropical and shows off my tan wonderfully!

7.30 a.m.: Into Make-up. Why can't a girl do her own? Because those heavy-duty studio lights turn you into a nightmare of bleached skin and deep shadows. This isn't a bit of lip-gloss and powder. This is the works: foundation cream, three different shades of powder, eyeliner... the lot.

7.15 a.m.: And make-up ladies are wonderful for a gossip. I wish I could tell you what the boys from The Bad Blades did the last time they were here!

7.30 a.m.: Thank the make-up lady for doing such a wonderful job on me. How does she make me beautiful? I ask, graciously. She says,"Oh that's nothing, luv, I had to do twenty zombies with gaping head wounds up on Bodmin Moor yesterday for the new horror series." Feel a little less full of myself.

8.00 a.m.: Into the studio for run-through of opening of the show and some other awkward bits. Goes OK. But...

8.30 a.m.: Programme Editor hates my new outfit. Says I should remember the show's called *Bright and Breezy* not *Teenage Airhead on Expense Account*.

8.31 a.m.: Burst into tears.

8.32 a.m.: Back to make-up

8.45 a.m.: Got to get into the studio. Can't find anything to wear. In desperation put on my old jeans and T-shirt. Serve him right!

9.00 a.m.: Programme Editor says he loves the new gear. Says it really shows I know how to connect with my audience.

9.15 a.m.: Warm up audience with story about my dresses. Feel happier in jeans anyway.

9.30 a.m.: On air.

While the adverts are showing the hubbub stops. That carefree, happy-go-lucky look on Daisy's face disappears. It's replaced with a look of intense concentration as she studies her script and listens to updated orders through her hidden earphone. (Ted the Technician, not known for his political correctness, will have asked, "Got your deaf aid in then?") The boys from The Bad Blades are manhandled into place like another piece of scenery before being "miked up". Ted the Technician will ask, "Want to do this yourselves, boys?" before shoving his hand up the inside of their T-shirts. He's hiding the wire, which is attached to a microphone slightly bigger than a match head.

If the studio is almost unnaturally quiet, the gallery is most certainly not. If you want to get a first-hand jolt of the excitement that makes people want to work in live TV, come to the gallery.

This is the control room. It is long, narrow and dark. It runs the length of the studio and is high above it. The main light is from dozens of flickering screens. Like an art gallery there are pictures all over. But these are on one wall. And they're TV screens. Big screens, small screens, tiny screens.

There are probably five cameras on the studio floor; each one has its own screen in the gallery. There are screens showing the studio where the next programme is coming from. There are several showing what you're seeing at home. Screens for taped reporters. Screens for outside broadcasts.

Add a couple thrown in for luck and a few more to keep them company, that's a lot of screens.

The director and his team are lined in a row facing them. On their desks are lots of knobs and buttons. Behind them are a few more desks for the people who're in charge of the whole show. It always makes me think of the bridge of a starship on a science fiction movie.

But what you really notice is the noise. The director's voice is the loudest: he's choosing which pictures to show and telling the presenters what to do, but there are lots of other people shouting as well. Let's listen as the adverts come to an end.

Gallery gabble

Director's main assistant: Network coming back to us in ten. Five. Four. Three. Two. One. Cue Daisy.

Director: Daisy, Camera Five. Go now! Ready to go to wide on Camera One. Now. Good. Good. What on earth does Camera Five think he's doing? Daisy, back to Camera One. Cut. Good. Are we ready with the report on the boys' last gig? Well, where is it? Give me a single on Joe. Daisy, I want you to talk to Joe first.

Assistant two: Camera Four give me more of the guests. Wider. Wider. Camera Two I want you to get a close-up of the boys' Ratz T-shirt. Someone offer a single (1) on Joe. Not you Camera Two stay with the T shirt. Right, close-up of Joe on Camera Four. Press (2), we're going to overrun by thirty seconds at the end, can we have the extra time?

1: A single: a shot just of Joe and no one else.
2: Press: Presentation – the people in charge of the people who say, "In an hour's time you can see the results when Jack flosses a tiger in *The Savage Earth* but first it's Daisy Mazey with *Bright and Breezy*. They can

Assistant three: Why are we not seeing anything on Monitor Seven? The report can't be in the gate (3).

.... They haven't finished the edit. Some problem with cut-aways. They need a few more minutes. And the front desk says the journalist from *Teen* still hasn't turned up.

Assistant four: Tell them we can give them another seven minutes, otherwise they've missed their slot... OK ...see if we can get the American satellite link-up right away... Tell Nadia she'll have to come up a little earlier. We want to go to her after this item.

let a programme go longer than it's meant to by a minute or two.
3: Gate. As in horses are in the gate ready to race. It just means the tape is in the machine ready to be played.

The horrifying thing about this for Daisy is that much of this babble is going on in her left ear as she's trying to sound bright and breezy.

It's certainly an action-packed day today: up-and-coming Nadia in New York on the latest craze — a gizmo that tells you if your pet is happy or sad, and has *Teen Magazine* really gone too far this time with its sponsored Snogathon? But before we go behind the bike sheds here are the boys from The Bad Blades.

If she's opted for "open talk back" rather than "switch" she'll hear absolutely everything, but only presenters with ice instead of blood ask for that... Even so she's listening to much of it while she speaks. This is why.

It's pretty unusual for two dance DJs to go on tour with a Death Metal band like Ratz, isn't it?

Joe: Well, we take stuff from all over for our sample and we're big fans.

> Director:
> *Camera Two, hold the T-shirt nice and steady. Stay with the logo if he moves around. Daisy! Joke about the T-shirt. When you want to. Soon as you can.*

Yes, I can see that: you're both wearing their rather gruesome T-shirts ...does the blood come out in the wash?

> **Director:**
> *Cut to Camera Two ...now! Even closer on the fangs! Right, pull out now. Good, Daisy. Hold that expression. Cut to Camera One to show her pulling a face.*

Thanks, Joe and Nick, ... let's have another word in a moment. Most of us remember your first hit "Sister Blissed Her". It was released two Christmases ago. And flopped before becoming THE big underground sound of last summer. But bet you didn't know that Nick first DJ'd at his uncle's wedding — when he was five — and Joe used to be in a band. A brass band. Don't blush boys, coming up some moments you might rather forget...

At least Daisy doesn't have to learn all of this off by heart. It's written and put on autocue. This is a big box, about the size of an ordinary TV that goes just underneath the lens. So she stares at the camera and reads:

There are just a few
words on every line
and as soon as you
have read the top
line it disappears
and
the next one comes
up.
This is so you don't
have to move your
head up and down
or from side to side.
You can see about
five lines at any one

time.
If
the
person
operating
it
goes
too
slowly
it
will
make
you
slow
right
down
and
sound
very
silly.

Make a box with your fingers and move them down the words, only showing a few lines at a time. Now do it too quickly: that's every presenter's nightmare. You end up speaking very fast gobbledygook.

Talking of fast gobbledygook, what's happening in the gallery?

"ETA[1] on the hack[2] another 20.

We can't get the Earlybird[3] up from America for another 10. Bad Blades are about to leave and there's 1.30[4] left on VT[5] and nothing in MCR[6]. Daisy just has to keep going. If we go to black[7] we're !$$!d[8] !!"

1 Estimated time of arrival.
2 The journalist from *Teen Magazine*.
3 A satellite transmitting pictures and sound.
4 One minute thirty seconds.
5 Video tape.
6 There are no tapes waiting to be played in the Master Control Room.
7 Your screen at home goes blank: the worst sin.
8 Couldn't hear this word but appears to be a technical term for "upset and in bad trouble".

As she chatters brightly and desperately Daisy looks around for something or someone to fill in the gap and spots...

Well, if it isn't my old friend, sitting in the audience — Peter Patterson. The last man to talk to Vincento Da Silli before he went into hiding after the caning the critics gave his last film! Come up here, Peter. How did he seem to you?

Well, rather desperate to avoid me, I suppose. One of his minders told me later that he persuaded the kitchen staff to put him in the bin and then they rather cruelly said that they ought to tip some of the rubbish...

And they chatter happily on. That's the way in TV. Think of all those celebrity chefs presenting gardening programmes, the TV newsreaders talking about their favourite fashions. Success breeds success. If a producer thinks you're good at being enthusiastic, knowledgeable and funny about one subject they'll think you can do it with anything else.

The biggest compliment you can get is that you "make good TV!" and you'll even love to learn the boys on bikes.